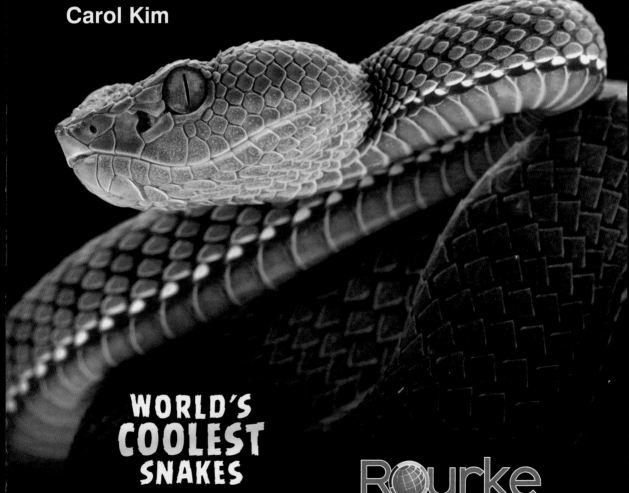

PIT VIPERS

Carol Kim

WORLD'S COOLEST SNAKES

Rourke
Educational Media

rourkeeducationalmedia.com

Fast Facts

Family: Viperidae

Pit vipers are a distinct group of snakes that fall under the viper family. This is a wide-ranging and varied group, containing 21 genera and more than 250 different species.

Subfamily: *Crotalinae*

Diet: Small mammals, birds, lizards, frogs, and other snakes

Range: Pit vipers live in North, Central, and South America, and parts of Asia.

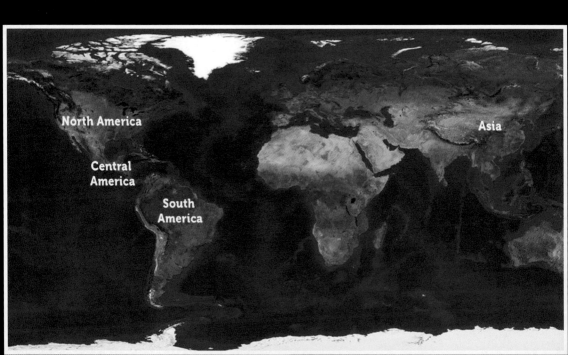

North America

Central America

South America

Asia

Table of Contents

Fanged and Dangerous

Pit vipers are some of the most feared and deadly **venomous** snakes in the world, but they are fascinating and extraordinary creatures.

Triangular Means Trouble

All pit vipers are characterized by a triangle-shaped head and a pair of long, hollow fangs. Venom is stored in a gland in the back of the upper jaw.

There are many kinds of pit vipers—more than 250 species exist around the world. Only snakes that possess unique heat-sensing pits are classified as pit vipers. These pits, located between the nostril and eye, can detect tiny differences in temperature given off by warm-blooded animals.

Tropidolaemus Wagleri

It's the Pits

Despite their tiny size, the pits house an amazingly complex tool.

The pits can detect heat by using thousands of specialized nerve cells. The heat signals form an image in the pit viper's brain that it uses to locate its prey with amazing accuracy, even in total darkness. They also help these snakes identify and protect it from larger **predators**.

Watch Out!

To watch a pit viper's strike, you better not blink, or you'll miss it. It only takes these snakes about 50 to 90 milliseconds to strike their target. Blinking takes about 202 milliseconds, over twice as long.

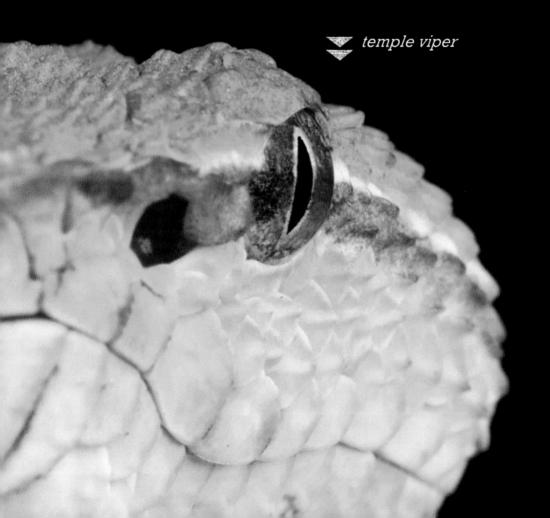

temple viper

Home Ssssweet Home

The various species of pit vipers live in habitats ranging from tropical rainforests to hot, dry deserts.

Some are ground dwellers, living under rocks and leaves, while others prefer the branches of trees. One, the cottonmouth, lives part-time in water.

Stay Away!

Ilha da Queimade Grande, or "Snake Island," off the coast of Brazil is no tourist destination. The only home to 4,000 highly venomous golden lancehead snakes, you could encounter one every few steps. Hardly a relaxing experience!

Fact or Fiction?

The most venomous pit vipers are found in Australia.

FICTION! While Australia is home to some of the most dangerous snakes in the world, no pit vipers live on the entire continent.

cottonmouth

golden lancehead

Frightening yet Beautiful

Pit vipers can look many different ways.

Sizes range from the foot-long (30.48 centimeter) hump-nosed viper to the massive bushmaster, which reaches lengths of 12 feet (3.7 meters).

Many pit vipers have skin colored in subtle earth tones, keeping them well **camouflaged** among rocks and leaves. But some species, such as palm pit vipers, are quite dazzling. They have vibrant yellow, green, purple, or even pink skin.

white-lipped island pit viper

Fruit with Fangs

Eyelash palm pit vipers prefer living in trees. These **arboreal** snakes wait for prey partially suspended by wrapping their **prehensile** tails around tree branches. Their bright coloring deceives birds, such as hummingbirds, into mistaking them for tropical flowers or fruit.

eyelash palm pit viper

◄◄ *Eyelash palm pit vipers get their name from the raised scales above their eyes that look like eyelashes.*

mangrove pit viper

From Common to Exotic: Pit Viper Species

Some pit vipers are commonly known, such as rattlesnakes, copperheads, and cottonmouths (also known as water moccasins). They live mainly in North America.

Central and South America are home to eyelash palm pit vipers, lanceheads, and bushmasters. Species found in Asia include the Malayan, hump-nosed, and Wagler's pit vipers.

copperhead

Final Steps

The sharp-nosed pit viper of China, northern Vietnam, and Taiwan is commonly called the "hundred pace snake." Why? Because according to locals, once bitten, victims can only manage to walk 100 paces before succumbing to the snake's venom.

sharp-nosed pit viper

Fearsome Fangs

Pit vipers carry a pair of long, hollow, **hinged** fangs that lie folded against the roof of their mouth. When they strike, the snakes open wide and hinge their fangs outward, piercing their prey and injecting venom into the victim.

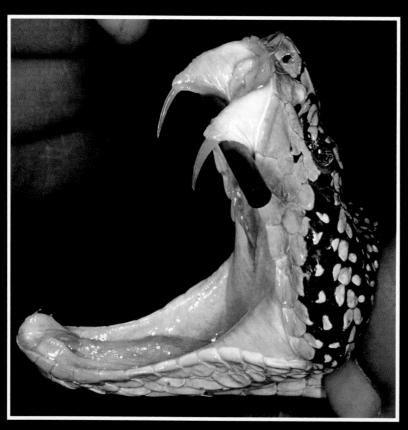

 Because their fangs lie folded when not in use, pit vipers have the longest fangs of all venomous snakes.

Lost Tooth? No Problem!

A pit viper strike is fast and violent. Sometimes a fang is lost or broken, but the snake is not toothless for long. It carries replacement fangs in the roof of its mouth, which move forward when one is lost.

rattlesnake

Fact or Fiction?

Pit vipers use all the venom in their glands with each bite.

FICTION! Pit vipers can control how much venom they inject. They can release venom from one fang, both, or none. Bites with no venom are called "dry bites."

Lethal Weapon: Venom

The venom of pit vipers varies among the different species. All have a toxic mix of **enzymes** and proteins that wreak havoc in their victims.

After striking, pit vipers quickly release their prey. The animal wanders off, but death comes quickly. The snake tracks the animal's scent to find it and swallow it whole.

Lizards such as geckos make a good meal for the smaller species of pit vipers.

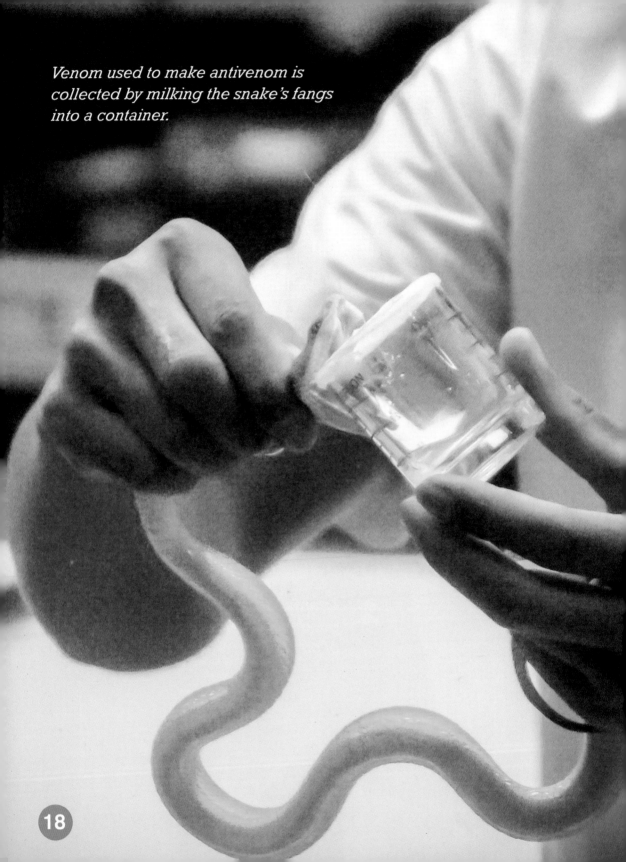

Venom used to make antivenom is collected by milking the snake's fangs into a container.

Worldwide, about 100,000 people die each year from venomous snake bites.

The most effective treatment is **antivenom** (or antivenin). It is made by injecting an animal, such as a horse or sheep, with harmless amounts of venom, triggering the production of antibodies. The animal's blood is then used to make antivenom.

Snakes must be milked many times to get enough venom to make antivenom.

Virtues of Venom

Venom has some beneficial uses. Brazilian pit viper venom has been used to develop medicine to treat high blood pressure. Scientists are exploring other possible medical uses of venom, such as pain killers and cancer drugs.

What's for Dinner?

Most pit vipers are **nocturnal**. They sit and wait patiently at night until prey wanders near and they ambush it with a sudden strike. They eat small mammals, birds, lizards, frogs, and even other snakes.

It will take this eyelash palm pit viper days, and sometimes weeks, to digest its prey.

Some pit vipers use the colored tip of their tails to mimic a worm-like creature and attract prey. This practice is known as caudal luring. An unsuspecting mouse may approach looking for a meal, but becomes one instead.

white-lipped island pit viper

Hunters as Prey

Pit vipers have many enemies. Birds of prey, such as eagles, hawks, and owls, eat pit vipers. So do some mammals, such as badgers, skunks, and raccoons. Other snakes are also common predators.

Kingsnakes overcome their victims by squeezing them to death.

Venom-Proof Snake

Kingsnakes are highly resistant to venom, which aids their ability to hunt pit vipers. They commonly eat rattlesnakes, copperheads, and cottonmouths. They can easily capture and devour snakes larger than themselves.

Pit Viper Babies: Cute But Deadly

Most snakes reproduce by laying eggs, but pit vipers largely give birth to live young. They are ovoviviparous, meaning the females carry the eggs inside their bodies. After hatching, the young emerge fully formed, leaving the shells inside the mother.

There are some oviparous, or egg-laying, pit viper species. These include the bushmaster and the Malayan pit viper.

Bushmaster females typically lay 10 to 12 eggs at a time.

Bird-Like Behavior

Many pit vipers that lay eggs will stay with the eggs and guard them by coiling their body around them. Mothers will not leave their eggs until they hatch, not even to hunt for food.

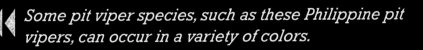

◀◀ *Some pit viper species, such as these Philippine pit vipers, can occur in a variety of colors.*

Fact or Fiction?

Male pit vipers battle over females.

FACT! Males will twist and turn about one another, sometimes for hours, each trying to force the other to the ground, to win the right to mate with a female.

The battle for mating rights is often called "the dance of the adders."

This young Vogel's green pit viper was likely one of about 10 babies. Pit vipers give birth to broods ranging from two to more than 80, depending on the species.

Males Need Not Apply

Female pit vipers are capable of giving birth to offspring without first being **fertilized** by a male. This process is called parthenogenesis. Pit vipers are one of a few animals that can reproduce this way.

Sharing Space with Pit Vipers

Pit vipers are often needlessly killed out of fear and ignorance. Yet they serve an important role in our environment, helping control populations of rodents and other pests.

The better these magnificent creatures are understood, the more they can be appreciated and protected.

Do Not Disturb

Fear of snakes is largely unfounded. Generally, pit vipers will not bite humans unless they feel threatened. They prefer to be left alone and most are afraid of people.

Fact or Fiction?

Newborn pit vipers are just as dangerous as adults.

FACT! Pit viper babies are fully venomous and able to inject venom into victims soon after they are born.

Glossary

antivenom (an-ti-VEN-uhm): a medicine used to treat the effects of venomous snake bites

arboreal (ahr-BO-re-al): living in or often found in trees

camouflaged (KAM-uh-flazhd): when something is disguised so that it blends in with its surroundings

enzymes (EN-zymes): proteins produced by plants or animals that cause chemical reactions to occur inside

fertilized (FUR-tuh-lized): when reproduction has begun in an animal or plant after causing the sperm cell to join with an egg cell or pollen to come into contact with the reproductive part of the animal or plant

hinged (hinjd): when two parts are attached to a joint that allows them to open and close easily

nocturnal (nahk-TUR-nuhl): active at night

predators (pred-uh-turz): animals that live by hunting other animals for food

prehensile (pree-HEN-sihl): adapted for grabbing or holding on to something

venomous (VEN-uhm-us): an animal that uses poison for hunting or defense

Index

Show What You Know

1. Explain the role of heat sensing pits in hunting prey.

2. What type of prey do pit vipers hunt?

3. Name some possible uses of pit viper venom.

4. Describe some hunting techniques used by pit vipers.

5. What are the different ways pit vipers give birth to young?

Further Reading

Discovery Channel, *Discovery Snakeopedia: Complete Guide Plus Lizards & More Reptiles*, Discovery/Time, 2014.

Mattison, Chris, *Snake*, DK Publishing, 2016.

Pressberg, Dava, *Vipers (Snakes on the Hunt)*, Rosen, 2016.

About the Author

Carol Kim has long been fascinated by all creatures found in nature, from cuddly sloths to scaly reptiles. She lives with her family in Texas, home to one of the largest rattlesnake populations in the U.S. She writes both fiction and nonfiction for children.

Meet The Author!
www.meetREMauthors.com

© 2019 Rourke Educational Media

www.rourkeeducationalmedia.com

PHOTO CREDITS: Cover & Title Page ©Matthijs Kuijpers / Alamy Stock Photo, Pg 5 ©CalDezign, Pg 6 ©reptiles4all, Pg 7 ©By Vince Adam, Pg 9 ©By Joe Farah, ©Nayeryouakim, Pg 10 ©By reptiles4all, Pg 11 ©Lee Grismer, ©KCHAE0, Pg 13 ©By Dennis W Donohue, ©discpicture / Alamy Stock Photo, Pg 14 ©ephotocorp / Alamy Stock Photo, Pg 15 ©Tee-roy, Pg 16 ©Mark Kostich, Pg 18 ©Kwhisky, Pg 19 ©Kwhisky, Pg 20 ©By Edvard Mizsei, Pg 21 ©Lee Grismer, Pg 22 ©By Matt Jeppson, Pg 23 ©Kyslynskyy, Pg 24 ©Avalon/Photoshot License / Alamy Stock Photo, Pg 25 ©MShieldsPhotos / Alamy Stock Photo, Pg 26 ©By Gary Mc Alea Photography, Pg 27 ©Rapeepong Puttakumwong / Alamy Stock Photo, Pg 28 ©Maxfocus, ©By muhamad mizan bin ngateni,

Edited by: Keli Sipperley
Cover design by: Kathy Walsh
Interior design by: Rhea Magaro-Wallace

Library of Congress PCN Data

Pit Vipers / Carol Kim
(World's Coolest Snakes)
  ISBN 978-1-64156-482-3 (hard cover)
  ISBN 978-1-64156-608-7 (soft cover)
  ISBN 978-1-64156-721-3 (e-Book)
Library of Congress Control Number: 2018930701

Rourke Educational Media
Printed in the United States of America,
North Mankato, Minnesota